Multi-Sensory Prophets

15 ready-to-use sessions on God's messengers
– for creative churches and small groups

Mike Law

MULTI-SENSORY PROPHETS by Mike Law
Scripture Union, 207–209 Queensway, Bletchley, MK2 2EB, UK
e-mail: info@scriptureunion.org.uk
www.scriptureunion.org.uk

Scripture Union Australia: Locked Bag 2, Central Coast Business Centre, NSW 2252
www.su.org.au

ISBN 978 1 84427 258 7

First published in Great Britain by Scripture Union 2007

© Mike Law

Cover design by waldonwhitejones of Basildon, Essex, UK

Internal page design by Creative Pages: www.creativepages.co.uk

Printed and bound by goodmanbaylis, The Trinity Press, Worcester and London

Scripture Union is an international Christian charity working with churches in more than 130 countries providing resources to bring the good news about Jesus Christ to children, young people and families – and to encourage them to develop spiritually through the Bible and prayer. As well as coordinating a network of volunteers, staff and associates who run holidays, church-based events and school Christian groups, Scripture Union produces a wide range of publications and supports those who use their resources through training programmes.

Contents

Making the most of Multi-Sensory Prophets

When the book and then the film of *The Da Vinci Code* took the world by storm, it seemed that everyone was interested in cryptic prophecies and mysterious messages. In this small-group resource we turn to prophecies not invented by men – but inspired by God. The prophets we will look at, and the messages they gave, firstly shaped a nation – but subsequently shaped a world.

Multi-Sensory Prophets is designed to help a small group explore what the Bible has to say about prophets and prophecy through a variety of experiences using the senses. This is a huge topic and so the sessions are wide-ranging rather than narrowly focused. Whenever you find a topic which interests and excites your group, then pursue it. Don't feel you have to move on to the next item; the material is intended as a 'menu' from which you can select for your group.

Reading the Bible in and out of group times

Many small-group studies, including others in this series, focus on one short passage from the Bible. In exploring the prophets this is not really possible. Often there are large chunks to read, so it will be helpful to encourage your group to read the passages in advance of the session. Some sessions involve moving around the Bible quite a bit. If you have people in your group who don't find it easy to find their way around the Bible, give people plenty of time to find passages and look up references.

You will find it helpful to vary the way the Bible is read in the group. Some examples are given in the notes but you might like to try some of the following where no specific suggestions are made:

— Have different group members read the sections into which the NIV divides the passage.

— Read round the group, each person reading a paragraph.

— Where the passage is long, give someone a week's notice to prepare to read it to the group.

— Read the passage aloud together.

— Read it silently and individually.

— Listen to the passage from a cassette or CD of the Bible.

— Read it a second time from a less literal version like *The Message* or *The Word on the Street*.

— Dramatise the reading for a number of voices.

— Explore using background music from a CD with the reading.

— If you have access to PowerPoint, you could create a series of images which interpret the Bible passage. These could be projected or viewed on a screen where facilities allow, or printed out on sheets of paper pinned up around the room.

Using other resources

The assumption has been made throughout *Multi-Sensory Prophets* that in most groups at least one person will have access to the Internet and so a number of recommended resources can be downloaded. However, there are always other options for those who are not able or do not wish to work in this way.

Journalling

A key part of learning to listen to God through *Multi-Sensory Prophets* is using a journal; maybe even two journals. There are templates at the back of the book which should be copied and given to each member to make their own personal journal. The success of this will depend on gentle and regular encouragement to keep up what will seem, at times, to be a demanding daily habit – even though it need take only a few minutes. It will also be useful for the group leader to keep a group journal in which to record the thoughts, impressions and conclusions of the group each time they meet.

Starting out

How do we approach these studies on prophets and prophecy? With the idea that every word, thought, picture that is received and shared by a member of the group is a prophetic word from God? Certainly not. Our own imaginations and enthusiasm may easily run away with us. But, let us begin by believing that, in the midst of our own weakness and confusion and stumbling, we believe God will speak. To be sure about what is of God and what is only our own idea will need careful sifting and much humility. But it is a price worth paying if we learn to cultivate the habit of listening to God, if we gain confidence and skill in understanding what God is saying, and if we see changes in our lives and the lives of others as we respond to God in obedience.

These sessions are not just about acquiring information. They are about experiencing the very thing we are talking about – hearing God speak. This can be scary (take a look at Deuteronomy 5:25,26). So take things gently. Don't make periods of silence too long at first. Accept and affirm even stumbling attempts at sharing what God may be saying. Encourage a spirit of learning and growing together. You never know through whom God may choose to speak. It may be the most unlikely person (Psalm 8:2). Take a look at **Can I hear from God?** on page 12 which gives more on this.

Because of the journalling, listening and sharing elements of the material, this course will work best if you start at the beginning and work consecutively through the sessions at weekly or fortnightly intervals. However, if your church timetable doesn't allow for 15 sessions, you can be selective.

The 15 sessions in *Multi-Sensory Prophets* are built around a common 'menu' approach:

Getting connected (allow 10–15 minutes)

This ice-breaker will get everyone involved and sharing together from the very beginning. It is easy to see the value of this part of a session when a group is just starting out or when new people have recently joined, but even if you have known each other for a long time you will often be surprised at what you discover.

Touching God (allow 15–20 minutes)

Jesus encouraged his followers to engage with God through all their senses. For example:

> **Look** at the birds of the air – Matthew 6:26.
> My sheep **listen** to my voice – John 10:27.
> **Touch** me and see – Luke 24:39.
> Take and **eat**; this is my body – Matthew 26:26.
> She has done a beautiful thing (when Mary poured sweet-**smelling** perfume over Jesus) – Mark 14:6.

A small group is the ideal context for exploring multi-sensory worship.

Living Scripture (allow 40–45 minutes)

The aim is to search the Scriptures, but also to allow the Scriptures to search us. 'All Scripture is God-breathed and is useful for teaching, rebuking, correcting and training in righteousness' (2 Timothy 3:16). Come expecting to be encouraged, challenged, changed.

The **Living Scripture** questions are based on the NIV (New International Version), but try reading the passage from an alternative version sometimes. Different voices will help bring the text to life, so experiment by having several people read the various characters, or try acting out the parables from time to time. Take a few moments to pray that God will inspire your discussion before you consider the questions.

Reaching out (allow 15–20 minutes)

It is easy to skip over this part of the meeting, particularly if you have let an earlier section run on too long. A group that stops looking outwards will soon become stagnant. **Reaching out** often includes an idea for a social activity as a great way of drawing new people into the group. Plan one into your programme from time to time.

 ## Digging deeper

This will give you a reminder about your journalling.

Leading a group

Some people shy away from leadership because they feel they do not know enough about the Bible, but a good small-group leader is more likely to have pastoral gifts than an expert knowledge of Scripture. Here are a few pointers towards effective leadership. For more help, see my book *Small Groups Growing Churches,* Scripture Union, 2003.

Prepare well
Each of the sessions in *Multi-Sensory Prophets* includes a choice of material. Look ahead and decide which of the suggestions are right for your group. Many of the ideas require some advance preparation – sometimes needing to be done not just the night before but over a period of weeks – and I have flagged these activities up under the heading **Well in advance**... Have everything ready before people arrive so you can concentrate on making them welcome. Don't be afraid to use the material as a springboard for your own ideas. Add your own touches; mix and match activities to suit the particular needs of your group.

Pass it on
Sharing out responsibility for different parts of the meeting will strengthen the group. Work towards a rota where different people lead different sections each time. Meet in various homes so that everyone has the opportunity to practise hospitality (Romans 12:13). Appoint an assistant leader and let them run the meeting from time to time. If the group becomes too big to fit into one home, your assistant can start up a second group.

People-minded
Be people-focused rather than programme-driven. Hospitality is important. Timing is also important – start promptly and don't overrun. If you go on too late, people might think twice about coming back next time. Be aware of the quieter members and draw them in with a simple but direct question sometimes (eg 'Chris, what do you think?'). But be sensitive. If someone does not turn up, get in touch before the next meeting. The aim is not to pressurise people, but to let them know they matter.

Pray
Pray regularly – daily if possible – for the members of your group.

Finally
Many of the ideas in *Multi-Sensory Prophets* have been used effectively in all sorts of gatherings, large and small. You'll find most can be adapted for school assemblies, retreats, quiet days, camps, conferences, training events, church services, prayer meetings, etc. Step out and experiment. Let your imagination fly!

1 Moses: The pattern of a prophet

Deuteronomy 18:14–22

A session looking at what makes a prophet a prophet

What is a prophet? For some people, the word brings to mind some longhaired ascetic mystic who spouts messages so convoluted that almost anything can be claimed as fulfilling them. Others picture a steel-jawed visionary determined to bring to pass the things he sees.

There are lots of prophets in the Bible, both the Old Testament and the New. They are a pretty mixed bunch: a political leader, a temple assistant, a shepherd and a Pharisee among them. Most were men but some were women. Some mainly preached – often messages of judgement. Others were more 'Action Man' types. The Bible tells us a lot about some; others are just mentioned by name; plenty are anonymous. Most never had their words written down, or, if they did, they have not survived to the present. So, a pretty mixed bag. As we move through this series of studies we'll not only explore who they were and what they did and said, but what the implications are for us.

We start with Moses – not the first prophet in the Bible; think of Enoch, Noah and Abraham for example – but the person who first clearly shows us what prophecy is all about. The scene in Deuteronomy is the desert. Moses is preparing the second generation (the disobedient first generation having died out during 40 years in the wilderness) for entry into the Promised Land by rehearsing all that God had done and all he required of his people.

 Getting connected

It's in the stars
You will need: a selection of horoscopes from popular newspapers and magazines. Share them out and have a discussion. Why do horoscopes feature in most popular magazines and tabloid newspapers? Does anyone really believe what they say? How do you react when you read that prominent politicians, business people and entertainers consult personal astrologers before making key decisions?

Or

It's in the genes
Pass round the pictures that group members have brought of themselves as babies or children or the downloaded prints, and give everyone a chance to guess who these people grew up to be. How much of the adult can we see in the child? Can we look at children we know today and see signs of who they will grow up to be?

Touching God

Meditation

In an attitude of prayer, invite anyone to share briefly any experience in which God has spoken clearly or directly into their life. Afterwards, share in saying together the **Psalm 119 Meditation** photocopied from page 10. Everyone should say together the words in bold from Psalm 119:129–136. One person reads the other words in italic. This could be one or more individuals appointed in advance, or the group leader.

Pause after each section to reflect and listen. Soft background music and candlelight (or subdued light) are often helpful during meditation.

 Living Scripture

Ask someone to read aloud Deuteronomy 18:14–22. Perhaps they could stand up and 'preach' it as Moses might have done?

1 What are a prophet's responsibilities? On a flipchart or large piece of paper, brainstorm writing a prophet's job description together. Think about things like working conditions, availability, line of report…

2 How do we know if a prophet is a true prophet? Look particularly at Deuteronomy 13:1–5. How closely should we apply this to people today? What other test is there for a true prophet? (If you'd like pursue this question further take a look at 1 John, especially 1:5–10; 2:4–6,9–11; 3:18–20; 4:1–3,20,21; 5:1–4. John is writing his letter to protect the church from false prophets/teachers (2:26). Make your own checklist of 'How to test a prophet'.)

3 How did Moses' own life show him to be a prophet? How much of Moses' ministry involved predicting the future? How much involved explaining God's present will for his people?

4 Does the leader of a church need to be a prophet or have a prophetic component within her/his ministry?

 Reaching out

Pizza evening
Hold a DVD and pizza evening, perhaps inviting some people who are not already members of the group. Watch *Moses the Lawgiver*, *The Exodus*, *The Ten Commandments* or the Time-Life DVD *Moses*, and discuss everyone's perceptions about prophets past and present.

Or

Book or art review
Invite a small number of people – from the group or from outside – each to talk about a book they have read which they regard as 'prophetic' (in whatever way they want to define that word). Encourage everyone else to choose one of the books discussed and to read it over the next few months. Alternatively, you could ask someone to talk about the work of an artist or filmmaker who is producing 'prophetic' work.

Digging deeper

On pages 62 and 63 you will find templates for making journals which can be used for any or all of the 15 sessions of this course. To make up the journal, photocopy pages 62 and 63 back to back to make the cover; then copy page 63 double-sided for as many sessions as you need. Put these pages inside the cover, fold and staple. You will need to make one journal for each member of the group. Ask them to personalise the covers and to use the journal pages to keep notes between sessions.

After this first session, suggest that to ease them into the new habit of keeping the journal, group members should just add a few moments to their daily time of prayer and Bible reading or, if they are not in the routine of having a 'quiet time', to create a space of a few minutes whenever it's convenient in their day to be quiet and listen to God. Make notes about any thoughts that come to mind. Don't worry if they seem very ordinary!

From session 2 onwards there will be an option to spend some time each week listening to God and speaking out what God gives to everyone. Look ahead to **Can I hear from God?** on page 12 and explain to the group what you plan to do. Ask them to pray for the next session during the coming week. Give time for sharing any fears and concerns. Pray for an openness to God and a freedom with one another.

Postscript to group leaders

During this first session, don't get too hung up on the dangers of becoming a false prophet. As we seek to listen to God over the coming weeks and share what we hear with others, we'll get it wrong sometimes – perhaps more often than not. As long as we're ready to have what we say tested by others and to learn from our mistakes, that's no sin.

Psalm 119 Meditation

Your statutes are wonderful;
  therefore I obey them.
The unfolding of your words gives light;
  it gives understanding to the simple.
I open my mouth and pant,
  longing for your commands,

Lord, this is how we want to be. But it's so hard. Our minds drift as we read your Word. We struggle to understand. And when it comes to putting it into practice, there are so many difficulties and problems.

Turn to me and have mercy on me,
  as you always do to those who love your name.
Direct my footsteps according to your word;
  let no sin rule over me.
Redeem me from the oppression of men,
  that I may obey your precepts.

Yes, Lord, that's what we need and what we want. Stick with us when we mess up; keep pointing us in the right direction each time we drift away. Help us to value what you say more than what our friends, families and colleagues say.

Make your face shine upon your servant
  and teach me your decrees.
Streams of tears flow from my eyes,
  for your law is not obeyed.

Your presence, your blessing makes all the difference. We want to spend this time together in order to meet with you. We want to learn your will for our life. We want to have your heart for our world.

Make your face shine upon your servant
  and teach me your decrees.

2 Samuel: The listening prophet

1 Samuel 3:1 – 4:1

A session exploring how a prophet hears from God

How much *theological education* do you need to be a prophet? How *old* do you need to be? If we're using the term 'prophet' to mean an officially recognised post within Israel, clearly only men who had proved themselves would be recognised as prophets. But if we're asking how old do you need to be to hear God speak and take that message to someone else (the essence of prophecy) then the story of Samuel will be a good place to look for answers.

Samuel was a child born in answer to prayer and then dedicated to God. He grew to be one of the most significant religious leaders in Israel and was responsible for anointing first Saul and then David, in response to the people's demands for a king. We have moved forward in history to around 1075 BC.

 ## Getting connected

The sound of silence

If possible and practical, go outside the building where you are meeting. Stand in the street or garden and listen for a couple of minutes. After noting the most obvious sounds, listen for fainter and more distant sounds. Remember what you hear and share with others when you go back inside.

If you can't go out, listen in various parts of the building or even just in the room you meet in.

Or

Blast from the past

Use the 'golden oldie' game of Chinese Whispers. The first person whispers a reasonably complicated phrase to the second, who whispers it to the third etc. When it gets to the end of the circle of people, check out the final version against the original.

Or

What did they mean?

Share examples of mysterious, confusing or amusing things overheard such as part of a conversation on a bus or train, in a shop etc.

 ## Living Scripture

Allow the group plenty of time to read 1 Samuel 3 silently. Invite silent prayer that God will speak through his Word, then lead a spoken prayer for God to speak (such as, 'Speak, Lord, for your servants are listening') before opening the discussion.

1   At first Samuel assumed that the voice he heard was Eli's. How did Eli's advice enable him to be sure that it was God who was speaking? How do we know if/when God is speaking to us?

2   Samuel lived in a 'spiritual environment'. To what extent do our regular spiritual activities – reading the Bible, praying, going to church – affect our ability to hear God speak at 'special' times?

3 What obligation falls on the person who has heard God's voice? If we think God is telling us something about another person, should we immediately go and tell them?

4 Samuel passes the test (Deuteronomy 18:22; see also 1 Samuel 3:19). But some prophecies are not immediately fulfilled. Do we need to look for every word to be immediately and obviously true? How do we judge whether someone's ministry is from God or not?

 Touching God

Can I hear from God?

Sing some quiet worship songs together; then encourage one or two people to pray that God will speak to the group about the situations that they each face.

Prepare the group for silent prayer by suggesting that they relax; there is no need to get anxious or uptight if you don't hear from God on this occasion. Reassure them that if they don't hear from God, that is no reflection on their spiritual state. Suggest that during the silence everyone should take note of, for example:

— a verse of Scripture that comes to mind

— a song or hymn they think of

— a picture or image impressed upon them

— a strong thought or idea

Spend time (five to ten minutes) in silent prayer, listening to God, reflecting upon whatever comes to mind. Ask God:

— Are you speaking to me?

— What does this mean?

— How should I share it?

After an appropriate period of time, the leader should pray asking God to guide as the group shares their experiences. Make it clear that God is sovereign and will not necessarily give everyone (or in some cases anyone) something to share. To remain silent and 'test' what others say is as valuable a ministry as to share something you believe God has given you. Together share the thoughts and impressions that have come during the prayer time. Do not be too quick to say, 'This is the word of the Lord,' but share in humility and invite the group together to decide whether what different individuals have experienced has been from God or from their own thoughts and imaginations. Note that things that come from our *own* thoughts and understanding may well be of value to the group – and may be inspired or prompted by God.

Commit to think and pray over these 'messages' during the coming week and pick up the discussion next time you meet. Although there are no absolute guidelines, from my experience I believe that if God is speaking then it is likely:

— the verses/words/pictures will be beneficial and uplifting to the group. (This is obviously not true of every prophetic word, but God is usually gracious and gentle to beginners);

— different people will express the same truth in different ways;

— the truth expressed will resonate with one or more members of the group.

Important: It may be that someone in the group brings a message which clearly is not from God.

If this is because the person bringing the word is naive or hasn't really thought through what they are saying, then use the approach above to test it. Is this helpful? Does it agree with Scripture? Is God glorified? Encourage the group to practise discernment, while still being encouraging. Don't let getting it wrong once put someone off from trying again.

Sometimes there are people who have their own 'agenda' – conscious or unconscious – and they may – intentionally or unintentionally – hijack the session to pursue their own thoughts under the guise of 'This is what God is saying to us.' You will need to be pastorally sensitive but firm. Make it clear that you don't accept this as coming from God. It may be helpful to talk things over with the individual concerned outside the session and ask them not to bring up their 'hobby horse' issues.

A great book to read and to recommend to your group is

How can I hear from God?

by Gillian Peall

Published by Scripture Union

Do remember that although it is valuable to set aside time specifically to listen to God, often God speaks to us by 'interruption'!

Whatever options you choose from the **Touching God** section in future sessions, consider trying to make time each week to be quiet, listen to God and briefly record and discuss what God says through the different group members.

 Reaching out

From the lips of children (Matthew 21:16)
Arrange to meet with a group of children. If your group includes lots of parents, you have a ready-made group. Or ask the children's ministry leader from your church if you could arrange to join one of the children's groups that meet regularly. Ask the children to share – verbally or by drawing pictures – what they think the world will be like in 20 years' time. What do they think are the most important things we should be doing today to make the world a better place? What do they think God is doing in the world?

Or

Warning for today
Samuel was called to speak out about corruption at the heart of the religious life of God's people (Check out 1 Samuel 3:13 and 2:12–17). Work together in the group on either

– a three-minute computer presentation using something like PowerPoint, or

– a three-minute photographic collage presentation using digital camera images

designed to challenge the Church today about the dangers it faces from within. Look for an opportunity to present it to your own church.

 Digging deeper

Encourage group members to share journal entries from the past week. For the coming week, at the start of the time begin with a simple prayer such as 'Speak, Lord, for your servant is listening,' and again write down your thoughts.

As group members open up and share the things they believe God is saying and what they are recording in their journals, it is important to ensure that:

— … what people share is received graciously. It may be strange or banal – or even downright wrong – but the response from the group needs to be gentle and encouraging even when (or especially when) someone has got things wrong.

— … what people share remains within the group. Even when it does not seem particularly personal or sensitive or obviously confidential, what is shared should remain within the group unless permission is given to share it more widely.

Elijah's complaint to God – 1 Kings 19:14

The Message

> I've been working my heart out for [God] … The people of Israel have abandoned your covenant, destroyed the places of worship, and murdered your prophets. I'm the only one left, and now they're trying to kill me.'

> I've worked my butt off for you God! The Israelis have thrown out your Contract, trashed your altars, assassinated your couriers. I'm the last one standing, and now they're after me!

The Word on the Street Bible

The Youth Bible, New Century Version

> LORD God All-powerful, I have always served you as well as I could. But the people of Israel have broken their agreement with you, destroyed your altars and killed your prophets with swords. I am the only prophet left, and now they are trying to kill me, too.

3 Elijah: The fighting prophet

1 Kings 19

A session to explore the stresses and strains of being a prophet

Old Testament prophets were not supermen. They were ordinary human beings subject to the same temptations, stresses and strains as the rest of us. And since the powers-that-be frequently decided to go any way but God's way, then being the prophet who pointed out how wrong they were could be a pretty scary experience. Even when God pulled all the stops out to work a series of miracles, Elijah still felt that he had failed or God had failed him. Often the two feelings are intertwined. Even the triumph on Mount Carmel wasn't enough for Elijah, although for the time being it seemed to change the path of history and turn the nation back to God. So how does God deal with a prophet who thinks he (or God) is a failure?

Elijah rose to prominence during the reign of Ahab and his wife Jezebel, who were notorious for encouraging the worship of Baal and other gods and persecuting those who worshipped Yahweh, the true God. It's around 874–853 BC and we're in the northern kingdom of Israel. (The kingdom split into two, Israel and Judah, not long after the death of Solomon.)

 ## Getting connected

Fighting fit

Get hold of an aerobics or other exercise DVD. Without making it too strenuous, try some of the warm-up exercises together.

Or

Stress busting

Stand in a circle. Gently massage each other's shoulders.

Or

Relaxing

Each person takes one minute to 'advertise' their favourite way of relaxing. Does anyone's description persuade someone else in the group to want to try their method?

 ## Living Scripture

1 As a group (with your Bibles open if necessary) remind yourselves of the story of Elijah as it progress in 1 Kings 18, from the start of the drought to the encounter with the prophets of Baal. Then have someone read aloud 1 Kings 19.

2 Today we are familiar with Post-Traumatic Stress Disorder. People involved in traumatic situations such as soldiers in a battle or survivors of a tragedy can suffer mentally and emotionally as a result. (For background information, check the National Institute of Mental Health website – **www.nimh.nih.gov/healthinformation/ptsdmenu.cfm**) What were Elijah's symptoms? What were the components of God's treatment?

3 What was there about earthquake, wind and fire (all symbols for God's activity) that didn't match Elijah's need to experience God at this time? What was there about the gentle whisper that gave Elijah the insight into God's nature that he needed?

4 Share any experience you have, from your own life or that of friends or family, of burnout or trauma arising from the stresses of life and/or Christian ministry. How did the church and other Christians help (or hinder) recovery? Are there lessons in God's treatment of Elijah that we could apply to contemporary situations?

 Touching God

Tear it up

You will need: lots of newspapers; chunky felt-tip markers; made-up wallpaper paste; a bucket or bowl; Bibles; some plastic sheeting to protect the carpet.

Spread out the newspapers and take a few minutes to reflect on the varied stresses and strains of modern life. Using chunky felt-tips write in big letters across the various pages verses from the Bible which promise peace, joy and hope, offer encouragement or stimulate patience, perseverance or action. When you have finished writing, spread the newspaper sheets out again and take a few moments to contrast God's Word and the world's need. Then rip up the papers and put them into the bowl, mixing them with the wallpaper paste to create papier-mâché. Work together to shape it into something you feel represents a symbol of healing. Finish by standing around your wet and sticky symbol and commit to God in prayer all who try to bring healing to our messy world.

One person may like to take it home and, when it dries, paint or decorate it, bringing it back to use as a reminder in future sessions.

Or

Shout it out

You will need: enough photocopies of **Elijah's complaint to God** from page 14 for everyone to have one.

With everyone standing, take a few moments to imagine yourselves in Elijah's position, standing on the mountainside. If you have time, read out the context for this verse from 1 Kings 19:1 onwards or 1 Kings 19: 9b. Encourage the group to think about any parallels between his situation and ours. Then, select one or more of the versions on the photocopy, and start together reading out the verse, beginning very quietly and getting louder and louder until everyone is shouting.

When the shouting has reached the end of the verse, allow time for a few seconds of silence and then read out 1 Kings 19:15–18.

With everyone sitting, give time for silent reflection on the question: 'What are you doing here?' After a suitable period of time, encourage sharing of any answers.

And

Hearing from God

Take time to be quiet, listen to God, share what God gives, briefly discuss and record it.

 Reaching out

Energy!

Arrange to go out together to play football, tennis, bowls (or whatever sport you're into). If you're really ambitious (or suicidal!) choose paint-balling.

Or

Relaxing together

If you feel you need to be less energetic, decide to go together to a health spa for a sauna, massage or pampering session.

Or

Do it for others 1

Find out about facilities for mental health care in your area. Is there a home or daycare centre or a hospital ward to which you could forge a link? Your local hospital may well have a chaplaincy, which would be a good place to start. Find out how you could be involved in offering support and encouragement to patients and/or staff.

Or

Do it for others 2

The Society of Mary and Martha (Sheldon, Dunsford, Exeter, EX6 7LE: **www.sheldon.uk.com**) is a Christian community existing to provide support and care to Christians in ministry who are suffering from stress and difficulty. Find out about their work and commit to praying regularly for them.

 ## Digging deeper

Encourage group members to share any journal entries from the past week. For the next week, identify one person each day who is in some kind of Christian ministry. Think about them in your listening time; hold them up before God. Record their names and any thoughts.

Postscript to group leaders

Be alert for members of the group identifying that Elijah's problems mirror their own. Thinking about this may have raised hurts and resentments, but perhaps no confidence to share their situation in the group. Try to speak privately with them to offer help, support and prayer.

4 Elisha: The seeing prophet

2 Kings 6:8–23

A session exploring how prophets see the world from God's perspective

Prophets are people who see things differently. They see from God's perspective. In the Old Testament there are a number of stories which demonstrate how prophets saw God at work, sometimes even in situations where it seemed God had abandoned his people. The prophets saw that God could choose to work through pagan kings as well as through his own people. The way in which Elisha, Elijah's successor, prays for his servant's eyes to be opened in this passage can serve as a picture of what prophecy is all about: showing the spiritual reality behind the temporal illusion.

There are two key areas in which it is helpful to see things from God's perspective:

– on the world stage, where the enormity of political, social and environmental concerns often seems too vast a context in which we might see God at work;

– in our own lives, especially at times when life overwhelms us and God seems distant.

Again we're in the northern kingdom. Elisha was speaking out over a time period of about 50 years in the second half of the ninth century BC.

 Getting connected

What can you see?

You will need: a computer logged on to a website demonstrating optical illusions – search Google for 'optical illusion' and choose from a wide selection. If you can't have a computer available in the room where the group meets, you could print off a selection of illusions. Alternatively, find some books of optical illusions from your local library to pass around. Talk about what we see and why we see it. For example, do you see the **Getting connected** symbol as two faces or a candlestick?

Or

Oops! Sorry!

Let the group share experiences of times when they have mistaken one person for another. How did they feel when they discovered that what they perceived as reality proved to be otherwise?

Or

Just for fun

You will need: a large drawing of a donkey pinned to a cork noticeboard or similar; a length of rope to represent a tail; a drawing pin; a blindfold.

Just for fun, play *Pin the Tail on the Donkey,* perhaps the version where you have to navigate the length of the room to reach the donkey, and think about the difference between where you *thought* the tail was and the reality.

 ## Living Scripture

Allow everyone a few minutes to read 2 Kings 6:8–23 from their own Bibles in silence and then tell the Bible story using the five-part script **Seeing and believing** from page 22. This story is a simple, historical account of events that happened long ago. But it provides insight on two levels: the world political scene and our own spiritual battles. Tackle either or both sets of questions.

Who rules the world?

1 Check out 2 Kings 3:1–3 to find out who was King of Israel at this time and what sort of king he was. 2 Kings 3:13,14 will give you Elisha's opinion of the king. Given that, why does Elisha provide such vital information to the King of Israel about what the King of Syria is doing? Do good kings have a monopoly on God's help?

2 What does 2 Kings 3:21–23 say about God's way of dealing with his enemies? Does it suggest anything to us about resolving situations of conflict?

3 If the ruler of a country today is a professing Christian (you can probably think of examples) does this mean that the country will be better governed? Do Christian rulers have a hotline to God?

4 What responsibility do we have as Christian citizens to support those in authority locally and nationally? How can we work this out in practice? (You might want to look at Romans 13:1–7 and/or 1 Timothy 2:1,2.)

Or

Who is fighting our battles?

1 Look through 2 Kings 6:8–23, noting all the references to seeing and blindness, guidance and being led. What does the story say about the sovereignty of God in revealing or hiding the truth?

2 When all we can see are the forces (of whatever kind) ranged against us, how could we have our eyes opened to see the situation as God sees it? If you were Elisha's servant, how might this experience have changed the way you looked at things in the future?

3 If God is the one who opens eyes and blinds them (verses 17,18) then, in situations of difficulty, should we expect God to give clarity of vision and understanding to his Church while confusing the understanding of those who oppose him?

4 Prophets were often concerned with the moral and social issues of their day. Think about a topical issue in your society, such as binge drinking or teenage pregnancy. What might be the dangers of being totally convinced that the way *we* see things is the way *God* sees things? While retaining a firm belief that God does guide and enlighten, what safeguards can we have against claiming our own ideas as God's ideas?

Touching God

Before and after

Use the photocopies of the old hymn *Lord, I was blind* from the opposite page as a meditation. Have two large sheets of paper or card and some pens available. Label one sheet 'BEFORE' and the other 'AFTER'. One person should read the hymn slowly, allowing one or two minutes after each pair of lines for members of the group to write or draw on the 'BEFORE' side (after the first two lines of each verse) or the 'AFTER' side (after the second two lines of each verse.) Don't write whole sentences, just a word or two; or sketch a simple symbol or line drawing that reflects the 'before' and 'after' of meeting Jesus. Afterwards, take time to examine the things that have been written. You might want to briefly share answers to the question: 'What new things do I need to see, hear, speak, live?' Pray for one another, based on the things that are shared.

Or

Praise

Sing one or more of these, as appropriate to where your discussions have taken you:

— Light of the world, you stepped down into darkness (© 2000 Kingsway's Thankyou Music)

— Great is the darkness (© 1992 Kingsway's Thankyou Music)

— Darkness like a shroud / Arise, shine, your light has come (© 1985 Kingsway's Thankyou Music)

— Immortal, invisible, God only wise

— Light has dawned that ever shall blaze (© 1988 Make Way Music)

— Like a candle flame (© 1988 Make Way Music)

Or

Prayer for those in power

You will need: collected newspaper photos of people of influence locally, nationally, globally.

How do we perceive those in leadership in our nation? In our world? How might God see them? Spend some time praying for key influencers on the national and global scene, sharing out the newspaper photos and working in twos or threes. Include people such as: the Queen and the royal family; the prime minister, the leader of the opposition and other national and local politicians; powerful people in industry, commerce, health, education; judges; the police; the Secretary-General of the UN.

And

Hearing from God

Take time to be quiet, listen to God, share what God gives, briefly discuss and record it.

 Reaching out

Who rules the world?

As a group, write a letter of support and encouragement to a prominent person who is campaigning for an issue which you support. For information on current debates and viewpoints of MPs, a useful website is www.TheyWorkForYou.com

Or

Who is fighting our battles?

Identify someone known to the group who is fighting some tough battles at present. Discuss the most appropriate way to show them support and encouragement – anything from sending a card to taking them out for a meal or offering to do some DIY! – and plan to put it into practice.

 Digging deeper

Encourage group members to share any journal entries from the past week. For the coming week, suggest that time be made each day for silent reflection on a different aspect of life, asking God to open your eyes to see it in a new way. Suggested topics:

Day 1 – Your family; Day 2 – Your work (paid or unpaid); Day 3 – TV; Day 4 – Your home; Day 5 – Your newspaper; Day 6 – Your church; Day 7 – Your friends.

Before and **after**

Lord, I was blind; I could not see
In Thy marred visage any grace;
But now the beauty of Thy face
In radiant vision dawns on me.

Lord, I was deaf; I could not hear
The thrilling music of Thy voice;
But now I hear Thee and rejoice,
And all Thine uttered words are dear.

Lord, I was dumb; I could not speak
The grace and glory of Thy name;
But now, as touched with living flame,
My lips Thine eager praises wake.

Lord, I was dead; I could not stir
My lifeless soul to come to Thee;
But now, since Thou hast quickened me,
I rise from sin's dark sepulchre.

For Thou hast made the blind to see,
The deaf to hear, the dumb to speak,
The dead to live; and lo, I break
The chains of my captivity.

William Tidd Matson, 1833–99

Drama script:

Seeing and believing

Narrator	The King of Syria was at war with Israel. After consulting his officers, he chose a place to set up camp. But Elisha, God's prophet, sent a message to the King of Israel.
Elisha	Don't go near that place! The Syrians are waiting in ambush there.
Narrator	Naturally, the King of Israel checked it out and warned his men to be on guard to avoid being surprised by an ambush by the enemy. In fact, this happened several times. Not surprisingly, the King of Syria was angry. He wondered if he was being betrayed by one of his own officers. He called them together.
King of Syria	Which one of you is playing for the other side?
Officer	Don't blame us, Your Majesty. It's the prophet Elisha. Elisha tells the King of Israel everything. I bet he even tells him what you say in the privacy of your own bedroom!
King of Syria	Find out where this Elisha is – and bring him in.
Narrator	A report came that the prophet was in Dothan. So the king sent a large contingent of men with horses and chariots to surround the city by night. Early the next morning, Elisha's servant was out early – and spotted the enemy forces.
Servant	The city is surrounded – and the word is that they're coming in to take you by force. We've had it! What can we do?
Elisha	Don't be afraid! There are more on our side than on theirs. O Lord God, open my servant's eyes. Let him see!
Narrator	God answered his prayer. When Elisha's servant looked up he saw that the hillside was literally covered with fiery horsemen and chariots. Then, when the Syrian troops attacked, Elisha prayed:
Elisha	O Lord, strike these men blind!
Narrator	Then Elisha said to the soldiers,
Elisha	You're in the wrong town. I know who you're looking for. Follow me and I'll put you on the right road and take you to him.
Narrator	In fact Elisha led them right into the hands of the enemy. It wasn't until they were close by the King of Israel's troops that Elisha prayed for their sight to be restored and they realised just where they were. The King of Israel wanted to put the Syrian soldiers to death, but Elisha persuaded him instead to treat the men kindly and to lay on a huge feast. The king complied – and after that incident the Syrians stopped attacking altogether.

5 Isaiah – The royal prophet

Isaiah 6

A session exploring the glory and majesty of God and his call to prophesy

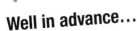

Well in advance…

In preparation for the activity **The wonders of his glorious love** make a collection of remnants of bright fabrics – especially scraps of velvet, silk, satins, sequinned material and so on. Also useful would be roll-ends of embossed wallpaper, glass beads, unusual wool, buttons, ribbons etc. See what you can scavenge from clever knitting and sewing people you know!

The prophet Isaiah, according to Jewish tradition, was of royal blood. He was certainly involved in prophesying to Judah's kings at the court in Jerusalem. He had a wife who also exercised a prophetic ministry (8:3) and at least two sons whose names had prophetic significance. It is perhaps no coincidence that this royal prophet has a vision of God as a great king; in the year that the earthly king dies he meets the eternal king.

If a prophet is someone who speaks God's words then we need to explore how prophets meet with God and hear from God – and Isaiah's call gives us a great opportunity.

Isaiah's ministry was from around 739 to 686 BC in the southern kingdom of Judah.

 Getting connected

Luxury

Start the time together by sharing Ferrero Rocher chocolates, if possible arranged in a pyramid on a silver plate. Or anything else you can think of which suggests sheer luxury – caviar and champagne, if you like!

Or

Incense

Using aromatherapy oils, incense or scented candles – or coffee and freshly baked bread! – create an enticing aroma in the room. Or have various smells available. Decide which you think is the most opulent.

 Living Scripture

1 What was the spiritual state of Israel at the time when Isaiah prophesied? Read Isaiah 1:2–4,10–17,21–23. Can you identify any parallels with our nation today?

2 Isaiah brought a message of judgement (5:3–7 and following verses), of invitation (1:18–20) and hope (2:1–5). How we do we balance these three elements in any message we might want to give to our nation?

3 Read aloud Isaiah 6. When the earthly king died, Isaiah saw the heavenly king; his call by the King of Kings enabled him to minister to earthly kings (Isaiah ministered to at least four kings, as it says in 1:1); the court of heaven inoculated him against the court of Judah. Does the

Church have any ministry to those in power today? What is it? How is it exercised?

4   Most of us feel that a closer encounter with God would be a great thing. Look again at Isaiah's reaction to meeting God (6:5) and God's response (6:6–8). Be honest with one another about how you feel about God dramatically breaking into your life – perhaps even during this group time!

 Touching God

The wonders of his glorious love. . .
Working together, create a banner or a mosaic that will express something of the greatness, holiness and loveliness of God. Use the brightest colours and most sumptuous of materials. Make it as large and spectacular as you can. You could use Isaiah 6:1–3 as the inspiration for your design.

Note: A hot glue gun is a quick and easy method of joining fabric and other materials – but take great care; hot glue on skin can do serious damage!

. . . And my own worthlessness
You will need: pens; photocopies of page 36; metal bin; matches.

Read aloud the verse from Elizabeth Clephane's hymn *Beneath the Cross of Jesus.* After a few minutes in silence, give everyone time to write below the verse the things they think of as their 'own worthlessness'. Gather up the papers, put them into a metal bin and set fire to them. As you watch them burn, read aloud together Isaiah 6:6–8.

And

Hearing from God
Take time to be quiet, listen to God, share what God gives, briefly discuss and record it.

 Reaching out

Visit
Arrange a visit to a cathedral or other building where the architecture gives a sense of the glory and majesty of God. Take time there to reflect/wonder/listen. Then talk over what the experience has said to you. Does the appearance of your church building create a positive atmosphere for worship?

Or

Calling
If God still asks, 'Whom shall I send? And who will go for us?' take time to reflect on what God is calling individual members or the group as a whole to do in response to the things you have been learning. What are the practical implications? What is the first step?

 Digging deeper

Encourage group members to share any journal entries from the past week and to continue with the journal during the following week. Suggest that each day the listening time could begin with the prayer, 'Lord, here I am, send me.'

6 Isaiah: The messianic prophet

Isaiah 40 and 52:13 – 53:12.

A session exploring the way prophecy points to Jesus.

Well in advance...

If you want to tackle the **Write it** activity, you will need to borrow some books on calligraphy from your local library.

Who can imagine a carol service without a reading from Isaiah 9 ('For to us a child is born… ')? Or the Easter season without a reference to Isaiah 53 ('He was despised and rejected by men… ')? Above and beyond all the other prophets, we see Jesus in the words of Isaiah.

 Getting connected

Shadow play

Position a lamp or powerful torch so that you can cast shadows on a wall. With the group looking at the wall, not towards the lamp, hold various objects up in front of the lamp. The group have to guess what they are from their shadows. You could also try the old trick of making animal shapes with your hands. (See **http://pbskids.org/zoom/activities/do/shadowanimals.html** for some ideas.) Discuss the 'clues' which helped you to guess correctly or misled you to a wrong conclusion.

Or

Pictograms

You will need: sheets of plain paper, felt-tip pens or coloured pencils.

Road signs use pictograms or symbolic pictures to warn us of what's coming up ahead (though what we're supposed to *do* about low flying aircraft or rocks tumbling down the hillside I've never been sure!). Create some life pictograms which could warn of:

— long sermon ahead

— holiday photos about to be displayed

— organist (or music group) hasn't had time to practise this week

— lots of messy activities in small group tonight.

 Living Scripture

You will need: pens; paper; concordances (some Bibles will have a mini-concordance in the back) Bibles or photocopies of Isaiah 52:13 – 53:12.

1   After allowing time to read the passage silently, each person should jot down whatever strikes them about the fulfilment of these words. After some time working individually, begin to share

answers. Using the concordances, try to find New Testament references which link to the verse in Isaiah.

2 Read Luke 24:25–27. Brainstorm as many examples as you can think of where the Old Testament (not just Isaiah) points ahead to Jesus.

3 The Old Testament speaks of Jesus hundreds of years before his birth, life and death. What significance does this have:

 – in confirming that Jesus is who he says he is?

 – for those prophecies which speak of Jesus' second coming?

4 In an age obsessed with mystical secrets – think of the global interest in *The Da Vinci Code* – how helpful is to refer to fulfilled prophecy in our evangelism and witness?

 Touching God

Messiah
Select two or three tracks of a CD of Handel's *Messiah* that are based on words from Isaiah: for example, 'Comfort ye, my people' or 'Every valley shall be exalted' from Isaiah 40 or 'Behold a virgin shall conceive' from Isaiah 7. If you don't have the words on a CD inlay card, you can find them together with the Bible references on the free Internet encyclopedia Wikipedia. Make yourselves comfortable and allow 10–15 minutes doing nothing but listening to the tracks. Allow the words and music to create images in your mind. Think about what being the Messiah means – the glory and the suffering. At the end of the music sit in silence for a little longer and offer up personal silent prayers of thanks to God.

Or

Communion
If your church tradition permits, share bread and wine or grape juice in a simple act of Communion together. If your church has a set liturgy you could use that; otherwise you could read from Isaiah 53:2–12 and Luke 22:14–40. Allow time for reflection on the way that God's actions in Old Testament days pointed forward to Jesus.

And

Hearing from God
Take time to be quiet, listen to God, share what God gives, briefly discuss and record it. This could effectively be incorporated into your listening to the *Messiah* or your Communion.

 Reaching out

Write it
You will need: pencils; erasers; a selection of pens of different types, sizes and colours (metal gel pens are good); pieces of stiff card folded like greetings cards; some books on calligraphy to serve as examples (borrowed from the library, or online examples can also be found at **www.fontcraft.com**).

Each person selects a card and creates a design on the front (in pencil first) based on one of the many names of Jesus. Or choose from the artwork on page 28. If you need some extra inspiration

CPO (Christian Publicity Organisation) has for many years produced Christmas cards based on the name of Jesus – you may be able to get samples from them at CPO, Garcia Estate, Canterbury Road, Worthing, West Sussex, BN13 1BW (**www.cpo.org.uk**).

Inside, write a message of encouragement based on a verse from Isaiah and send the card to someone who needs cheering up.

Or

Music evening

Plan an evening in which you play excerpts from a recording of Handel's *Messiah* alongside brief explanations of the Biblical texts on which the libretto is based, pointing out the prophecies and how they were fulfilled in Jesus. Invite friends and neighbours.

 Digging deeper

Encourage group members to share any journal entries from the past week. Each day in the coming week focus on a description of Jesus as you listen to God. If you have time, you could look up the Bibles verses here and then record your thoughts: Day 1 – Wonderful Counsellor: Isaiah 9:6; Day 2 – Mighty God: Isaiah 9:6; Day 3 – Everlasting Father: Isaiah 9:6; Day 4 – Prince of Peace: Isaiah 9:6; Day 5 – Holy One: Isaiah 49:7; Day 6 – Foundation: Isaiah 28:16; Day 7 – Refuge and Shelter: Isaiah 25:4.

Postscript to group leaders

For a comprehensive guide to messianic prophecies, take a look at *All the Messianic Prophecies of the Bible,* Herbert Lockyer, Zondervan, 1973.

Wonderful Counsellor

Mighty God

Prince of Peace

7 Jeremiah: The prophet of judgement

Jeremiah 1

A session exploring the way prophets speak uncomfortable words

Well in advance...

For **Cartooning**, collect cartoons on the theme of judgement – involving as many people in the group as possible. Search in newspapers, magazines and published cartoon collections. Ask someone to explore Gary Larson's *Far Side* work, *Pearls Before Swine* by Stephen Pastris and, by contrast, ask someone else to explore Matt's cartoons. **www.comics.com** is a useful site.

Jeremiah / n. a person who complains continually or foretells disaster. – *Concise Oxford English Dictionary.*

Jeremiah's name has come into our language as someone with a very gloomy outlook on life. It's true that Jeremiah had an unpopular message to proclaim and that he suffered personally in delivering it. But, as we shall see in a later session, he also had a strong message of hope.

Jeremiah was born into a priestly family, although it is unlikely he served as a priest. It was probable that he heard the call of God to prophesy in his teens. It was a costly and life-changing call to what might have seemed a futile task.

The resonance is clear. Our society may seem too big, too powerful, too entrenched to change. But God has put his Church into that society to bring his prophetic word.

In Isaiah's time, God delivered the southern kingdom from their enemies the Assyrians (Isaiah 37). One hundred years later the people have not changed their ways and God is preparing them for exile. Jeremiah's ministry was in preparation for the fall of Jerusalem in 587 BC.

 Getting connected

Which way are we going?

Divide the group into two teams. Give each team three minutes to come up with as many reasons as possible to show that their locality / country / the world (choose whichever they like) is becoming (team A) a better place or (team B) a worse place to live.

Briefly share your reasons and then take a vote on whether life is getting better or worse. What is the majority decision?

Or

Cartooning

You will need: cartoons; paper and pens.

Look at the cartoons collected by the group. Which is the funniest? Which has the strongest message? Do they say anything overall? Try your hand individually, in pairs or as a group at producing your own cartoons on the same theme. Don't worry about the quality of the drawing; it's the ideas that count.

Living Scripture

1 Jeremiah 1 tells us that God knew, set apart and anointed Jeremiah even before he was born. Is this true of us, to any extent? Check out Romans 8:29,30. To what have we been 'called'?

2 Jeremiah protests his inability (verse 6). How does God answer him (verses 9,10,17–19)? Use your imagination to put yourself in Jeremiah's shoes. How reassured would you have been? What might your fears have been? What are your fears now about being used by God? What reassurances do you think God is giving?

3 How can any human being have the power to *uproot and tear down, to destroy and overthrow, to build and to plant* (verse 10) the nations of the world?

4 Does the Christian message, whether proclaimed from the pulpit or from our own conversations and lives, need to include a warning of judgement? Or should we only share *good* news?

 Touching God

Muddy waters

You will need: a large, clear bowl of water (not too much water – you want to end up with thick mud); a container with earth in it; some flower seeds.

Set everything on a table in the centre of the group. One at a time, pick up a handful of earth and say, 'Lord, our society is polluted with … ' (complete however you think appropriate) and drop the earth into the bowl.

When you have finished and are left with a bowl of muddy water, offer it to God as a symbol of the society in which we live. Ask for his forgiveness, both on behalf of society and for ourselves as part of that society. Read the following words from Jeremiah and hear them spoken about our society:

> *My people have committed two sins:*
> *They have forsaken me,*
>   *the spring of living water,*
> *and have dug their own cisterns,*
>   *broken cisterns that cannot hold water.*
> *Have you not brought this on yourselves*
>   *by forsaking the LORD your God*
>   *when he led you in the way?*
> *Your wickedness will punish you;*
>   *your backsliding will rebuke you.*
> *Consider then and realise*
>   *how evil and bitter it is for you*
> *when you forsake the LORD your God*
>   *and have no awe of me.*
>
> Jeremiah 2:13,17,19

Drain most of the water out of bowl but leave the earth. Scatter flower seeds over it, choosing something that can cope with very wet soil, and put it in a place where over coming weeks you can see hope grow.

Or

Clay
You will need: a handful of air-drying modelling clay for each member of the group. As each group member moulds the clay to make a figure of themselves, read out the following passages:

Job 10:8,9
Isaiah 45:9 and 64:8
Jeremiah 18:1–10
Romans 9:20,21
2 Corinthians 4:7
2 Timothy 2:20,21

Note: If, as group leader, you are moulding your own clay, you'll need to have the passages copied out or risk covering your Bible with clay!

Mark each figure with the sign of the cross as a symbol of acceptance of God's plans and purposes for our lives.

And

Hearing from God
Take time to be quiet, listen to God, share what God gives, briefly discuss and record it.

 Reaching out

Write a letter
Write a letter to the local newspaper challenging something that concerns you in the local community. Work together to make it a Jeremiah letter: courteous, clear, courageous, brief and to the point – but possibly uncomfortable to read!

Or

Renewing vows
Jeremiah uses the picture of an unfaithful wife to illustrate Israel's unfaithfulness to God. Could your group organise a service of renewal of marriage vows for couples who have been married in your church? Discuss what would be involved. Who will talk with the church leadership / look at what is an appropriate date / send out invitations / organise a programme / take part in the event?

 Digging deeper

Encourage group members to share any journal entries from the past week. This coming week, listen to God at a point in your day immediately after watching the TV news, listening to the radio news or reading a newspaper. Record your thoughts.

JESUS in the Wilderness

IT IS WRITTEN
How has the Bible helped you to resist temptation?

THROW YOURSELVES DOWN
How have you been tempted to be the centre of attention?

IT'S ALL YOURS
How have you been tempted by promises?

BREAD FROM STONES
How have you been tempted by your appetite?

MOSES in

BURNING BUSH
Share an experience of hearing God speak

WATER FROM THE ROCK
How do you find spiritual refreshment?

Wilde
LI

JOHN in t

LOCUSTS AND HONEY
How does your lifestyle affect your walk with God?

PREPARE THE WAY
What led you to Jesus?

MANNA
How has the Bible come alive for you?

GOLDEN CALF
Share an experience of failure and forgiveness

RUNNING AWAY
Talk about a time you ran away or felt like running away from God

e Wilderness

ness

FE

ELIJAH in the Wilderness

STRENGTHENED BY AN ANGEL
What picks you up when you are down?

EARTHQUAKE, WIND AND FIRE
Have you ever looked for God where he can't be found?

STILL SMALL VOICE
How has God whispered in your ear?

Wilderness

TAX COLLECTORS AND SOLDIERS
What is the biggest challenge to your everyday life as a Christian?

ARE YOU THE ONE?
Are there times when you doubt your faith?

8 Jeremiah: The weeping prophet

Lamentations 3:1–33

A session exploring the prophet's reaction to the judgement he has prophesied

Well in advance...

For **Touching tragedy**, ask someone in the group to record a number of short TV news reports of war, famine or other kinds of human suffering that hit the headlines over a 2–3 week period.

The book of Lamentations has traditionally been ascribed to the prophet Jeremiah and he remains the most likely author. It is clearly the work of an eyewitness to the destruction of Jerusalem. It consists of five poems, the first four of which are written as acrostics – each stanza beginning with a different consecutive letter of the Hebrew alphabet. All the poems have a complex and sophisticated structure. They are not, therefore, a spontaneous outburst of grief, but rather a considered reflection on what God has done. Why are we looking at them in a series on prophets and prophecy? In one sense they are prophetic; the situation is not only seen as a man-made disaster but as somehow coming from the hand of God. But, perhaps more importantly for us, they bring home the enormity of our responsibility to bring God's Word to our society. No society is immune; the judgement that fell on Israel could fall on us.

Getting connected

Moved to tears (1)

Have each person peel and cut up an onion or, if it's impractical to do it then and there, pass around a cut onion in a bowl. Feel the sting of the onion in the eyes. Allow tears to run. Read aloud Lamentations 1:1–12. **Note:** it would be prudent to check first to see if anyone has any allergies.

Or

Moved to tears (2)

Share the film, book or play that has most moved you. What was it that brought the lump in the throat? What real-life situations have brought you to tears or close to tears?

Living Scripture

1 Have someone read Lamentations 3:1–18. If you knew nothing else about God, how would you describe him – based on this passage?

2 Read together aloud Lamentations 3:19–33. What difference does it make to your understanding of God's character, nature and actions that 'he does not willingly bring affliction or grief to the children of men' (verse 33).

3 Lamentations is a book of mourning. What role does the Church have in helping people to grieve?

4 There are contrasting ways of looking at tragedy, disaster and atrocity: either God is at work in

it or he is not. If God is not somehow *in* even the worst of atrocities, what is to prevent us from being overcome by the horrors of this world?

5 Tory MP Boris Johnson once famously accused the people of Liverpool of wallowing in grief (and had to apologise for it). What do the collections of flowers and toys at the roadside where a child has died say about our society? What prophetic word does the Church have for that situation?

6 Where does hope in the midst of disaster come from and how do we see and experience it (verses 21–30)?

 ## Touching God

Touching tragedy
You will need: a five-minute compilation of TV reports (see **Well in advance…**)

After you have watched the news reports, pray that God will give you renewed sensitivity to the things that are happening in our world. Then play the reports again, this time with the sound off, and pray aloud together for the things you are watching.

Or

Sing or listen
2007 is the 200th anniversary of the abolition of the slave trade in the British Empire. Listen to some of the voices of slavery on **http://memory.loc.gov/ammem/collections/voices/title.html** Play on a CD or sing some well-known Negro spirituals which evoke the experience of the slaves. Pray silently for healing of the past and freedom for the oppressed today.

And

Hearing from God
Take time to be quiet, listen to God, share what God gives, briefly discuss and record it.

 ## Reaching out

Campaigning
Slavery lives on! Up to 100,000 women are trafficked into Europe every year. Find out about the various campaigns seeking to prevent trafficking in people, especially women and children. In particular look at Stop the Traffik, launched by an alliance of Christian organisations. The website (**www.stopthetraffik.org**) gives lots of ideas, from signing a global petition to building a freedom wall. You could download their Stop the Traffik postcards and get everyone in the group to sign. If you live in the London area, find out about the Poppy Project, a Home Office initiative to provide support and housing to women trafficked into prostitution. Is there any way the group could be involved?

Mourning with those who mourn
People go on grieving long after the death of a loved one. Discuss the possibility of organising a service of comfort and hope for bereaved people. Open it to the local community, sending specific invitations to people who have been bereaved in the past 12 months. Go to **www.cofe.anglican.org/worship/liturgy/commonworship/text/funeral/memorialservice** for a

useful sample memorial service on which to build your own event. Provide tea afterwards. (Be prepared! In one city, 800 people turned up to such a service!)

Digging deeper

Encourage group members to share any journal entries from the past week. For the following week, each day when you take time to listen to God, start by focusing on a tragedy. You could include local, national or international tragedies, or forgotten tragedies.

_____

...And my own worthlessness

Beneath the Cross of Jesus

Upon that cross of Jesus
        Mine eye at times can see
The very dying form of One
        Who suffered there for me;
And from my smitten heart, with tears,
        Two wonders I confess –
The wonders of His glorious love,
        And my own worthlessness.

Elizabeth Clephane

_____

_____

_____

9 Jeremiah: The prophet of hope

Jeremiah 29:1–14

A session exploring the positive message of prophecy

Well in advance...

For **Symbols of hope**, ask all members of the group to bring something to this session which gives them hope. It could be a picture, a photo, a piece of music, some words, an object.

In the film *Clockwise,* the headmaster, played by John Cleese, says, 'I can cope with despair, it's the hope that gets me.'

The Jewish exiles were being given false hope by the prophets in Babylon: 'It's OK… this won't last… we'll soon be going home.' When hopes are raised, life is put on hold. When those hopes are dashed, life falls apart. So God, through Jeremiah, gives realistic hope:

— an assurance of his presence with his people in exile;

— a command to integrate with the Babylonian society;

— a promise that the time is coming when their grandchildren will go home.

If we are to be prophetic people, we need to be careful not to offer false hope ('Revival is just around the corner') but be clear that our message of hope really does come from God.

As for the context here, the exile happened in phases from about 605 BC. Likewise the return also occurred in phases, with the first groups going home around 537.

 ## Getting connected

Call My Bluff

Play a few quick rounds of 'Call My Bluff'. Three people each give different definitions of an obscure word, only one of which is true. The rest of the group have to guess the true meaning. Briefly talk about how we decide whether someone is lying or telling the truth. Which are we more likely to believe: an optimistic forecast or a pessimistic one?

Or

Home sweet home

You will need: felt-tip pens, large sheets of paper.

Giving them just five minutes, invite everyone to draw the place they've lived where they felt most at home. Then get them in twos and threes to describe why it was or is special. Does anyone still feel homesick for a place they have left?

 ## Living Scripture

Use your imagination. You are an exile from Israel in Babylon. The prophets are all saying this is just a temporary affair and you'll soon be going home. Take a few minutes to focus on the difference this hope makes to your life. A letter arrives from the prophet Jeremiah – the only prophet who correctly predicted the exile in the first place. Read Jeremiah 29. Now how do you feel? Who are you going to believe and why?

1 How do you pray for the peace and prosperity of a culture that regards your God as just one of many and is totally opposed to all the values and beliefs you hold?

2 If God's plans are for prosperity not harm (verse 11), why were the people in exile? Does the fact that God wants to work for good in our lives (Romans 8:28) mean that we will always have easy/happy/peaceful lives? Does success mean that we must be right with God? Or failure mean that we're out of step with him?

3 What does it mean in practical terms to seek God with all our heart (verse 13)?

4 Is the Church in your country a Church in a pagan land? If so, what should we seek from God? A return to the days when the Church was a key player in society? Or is there some other way? What prophetic message should we be delivering to the Church?

5 Are you hopeful or downcast about the future of the Church? Why?

 Touching God

Symbols of hope
Allow each person a minute or so to show what they have brought and explain why it symbolises hope to them. Listen to some of the music, look at the photos, handle the objects. Create a display on a table in the centre of the group if possible.

Then invite group members to write on a piece of card (folded like a tent so it will stand up) something they are hoping for. Add those to the display. Read aloud Jeremiah 29:11–13 and allow time for silent or spoken prayers.

Or

Words of hope
You will need: a magnetic poetry kit (These cost about £17 new and are available in bookshops, or through **www.shopboxuk.com**; Amazon sell used sets for as little as a couple of pounds); a metal sheet such as a baking tray (unless you prefer to do this gathered around the fridge door).

Spread out the magnetic word tiles on a table in the middle of the group alongside the metal sheet. Take turns to choose words that say something to you about 'hope' and place them on the sheet. When you have a couple of dozen words, as a group begin to move them about into sentences, adding other words as necessary. Aim to create four, six or eight lines of poetry. When you have finished, take time to reflect quietly on what you have created. Then pray short prayers of thanks to the God who gives hope, even in the midst of despair.

And

Hearing from God
Take time to be quiet, listen to God, share what God gives, briefly discuss and record it.

Reaching out

Picture postcards

You will need: pens; felt-tip pens; some local picture postcards or notelets or thin card folded into card shapes.

Send postcards, notes or hand-drawn cards to as many people as possible known to the group who are living away from home and may be feeling homesick. Write cheerful, fun messages, and sign them from the whole group.

Or

Give hope

Decide to do something practical as a group to give hope to another person. Can you send a gift to someone in need? Sponsor a child or a feeding programme? Write a letter or send some flowers to someone who needs encouragement?

Digging deeper

Encourage group members to share any journal entries from the past week. For the coming week, let thankfulness be your theme. Each day as you come to listen to God, take a moment to thank him for one good thing, large or small, that's happened anywhere in the world. Record your thoughts.

10 Daniel: The political prophet

Daniel 4

A session exploring the political dimensions of prophecy

Well in advance...

If you want to tackle the statue model in **Make a monster**, you will need to collect everyday scrap materials such as coloured foil and papers, cardboard tubes, remnants of cloth, bottle tops, pipe cleaners, yoghurt cartons etc.

For **Living Scripture**, encourage group members to read Daniel 4.

Jeremiah's instructions to the people to settle down in Babylon were certainly taken to heart by Daniel. He joined the civil service and rose to one of the highest posts in the land. And yet, although the story of Daniel is all about 'fitting in' in Babylon, it's also about knowing when to make a stand.

When everything about a situation seems black and white – where there are 'goodies' and 'baddies' – it's easier to make decisions. But often things are complex, and decision-making becomes much harder.

Daniel and his friends went into exile after the battle of Carchemish in 605 BC when various young men from noble families were taken to be trained up in the Babylonian court.

 Getting connected

Make a monster

Using modelling clay or plasticine, have a go at making the four beasts of Daniel 7. Or, using everyday scrap materials (see **Well in advance...**), have a go at making the statue from Daniel 2:31–33. Lego, if you can access enough, might be another option for making the statue.

Or

Success and failure

Divide the group into two and give each a pile of fairly recent newspapers. One group must find as many stories as possible which show government successes; the other as many stories as possible which show government failures. After five minutes have the groups show their stories and award points (1 to 5) according to how big a success or failure each story is. Add up the points at the end to give your verdict on the government. Is God at work through government initiatives?

 Living Scripture

Read Daniel 1.

1 Daniel and his friends would not compromise on the food they ate but were prepared to compromise by being trained to work for a foreign king. How might they have decided which compromises were OK and which weren't? Checking out Jeremiah 29:7 may help your discussion.

Read Daniel 4. This is such a long passage that it will be helpful if everyone has read it before the session. If not, get them to read it silently. Then have one person summarise the passage while everyone keeps their Bibles open. Then consider the questions.

2 Nebuchadnezzar is pretty hazy about who Daniel worships and follows (4:8,9). Nevertheless God interprets the king's dream to Daniel and Daniel interprets it to the king, despite it being bad news. What does this suggest about:

— God's sovereignty?

— Daniel's responsibility?

3 Why should God restore a king like Nebuchadnezzar rather than destroying him?

4 Dreams figure prominently in Daniel. How was Daniel able to interpret dreams? (Look particularly at 2:27,28; 7:15,16; 8:15,16; 9:1–3,20–23;10:2,3.)

5 Does God speak through dreams today? If so, how are we to understand them? Have any of the group had a dream they believe was from God?

6 In seeking Old Testament examples or parallels to guide us in twenty-first-century living, should we regard ourselves as living in Israel or Babylon? What difference does it make?

 Touching God

Role play
Role play a situation where a Christian is arguing the case for being able to wear a cross at work and an employer is trying to enforce a 'no religious jewellery' policy. After watching the role play, choose some passages of Scripture for each of the characters to reflect on. Share real-life situations group members face where decisions between conflict and compromise have to be made and prayerfully seek God's word for those situations.

Or

A picture of God
You will need: large sheets of paper; coloured pens, pencils or paints; Blu-tack or plastic sheeting or similar to protect the workspace if needed.

Invite someone to read aloud Daniel 7:9,10 two or three times. Using the paper either spread on the floor or tacked onto the wall, encourage everyone to draw something pictorial or abstract that expresses what they have just heard. Discourage a literal representation of the verses and make the point that this is not about artistic gifts.

Afterwards, look at each other's work and share comments about what you see of God in each picture. Finish with a time of prayer that praises God for who he is.

And

Hearing from God
Take time to be quiet, listen to God, share what God gives, briefly discuss and record it.

Reaching out

Clash of cultures?

Encourage group members to make contact with someone in their locality who is relatively new to the country. Invite them for a coffee. Without being confrontational, talk about the cultural differences they are experiencing. What have they found most shocking? What is hardest to come to terms with? What was better than expected?

Allow time to share experiences at a future group meeting. What have you learned?

Or

Contact your MP

Write as a group to your local MP(s). Thank them for the work they do. Tell them that you are praying for them (make sure you are!). Ask them what their needs and concerns are. Ask how they feel local churches can best help enhance the life of the community and the country.

Or

Campaigning

Find out more about the political involvement of your own denomination and/or the Evangelical Alliance (**www.eauk.org**).

 Digging deeper

Encourage group members to share any journal entries from the past week. This coming week suggest that everyone takes time to listen to God immediately before they go to sleep. In the morning, record any dreams you've had.

Postscript to group leaders

If you choose to write to your MP(s), you may be pleasantly surprised by the response you receive – so be prepared to meet up with them or receive them at a church service or some other activity of the church.

11 Hosea: The forgiving prophet

Hosea 1:1 – 3:5 and 11:1–11

A session exploring God's grace to people who've abandoned him

Well in advance…

For **Making our vows**, track down someone in the group who's willing to bring along a video of their wedding.

Hosea prophesied at a time when Israel had turned from God to worship idols. Israel's unfaithfulness is pictured in the way Hosea's wife Gomer abandons him. But, remarkably, the story doesn't end there. Hosea seeks out Gomer and buys her back from a life of slavery. It's one of the most powerful pictures of God's grace anywhere in the Old Testament. In a very daring way Hosea shows us the hurt in the heart of God when his people are unfaithful and the amazing lengths to which God will go to bring about a reconciliation which his people do not deserve and often don't even seem to want.

After looking at the southern kingdom in exile we are now back in the northern kingdom in the second half of the eighth century BC – roughly around the time Isaiah was prophesying in the south.

 Getting connected

Across a crowded room
If you have any married or engaged couples in your group, ask them to role play or describe their memory of their first meeting or their first date. Do these memories fit in with people's preconceptions of romantic encounters?

Or

Young people today
Download the Monty Python sketch *The Four Yorkshiremen* from **www.phespirit.info/ montypython/four_yorkshiremen.htm**. If your group remember it well you may not need the script; if they don't know it then read it to them.)

Then try to create your own sketch about how well-behaved young people were 'in my day' and how badly behaved they are today. One member of the group should describe how young people today behave. Each person then contrasts that with a statement 'when I was young' – each statement being more exaggerated in order to outdo the one before.

Here's an example:
- 'Young people today – always talking on mobile phones.'
- 'Talking on mobile phones! When I was young we were only allowed to speak when we were spoken to.'
- 'Speak when you were spoken to! When I was young we had to grovel on our knees when we were spoken to.' And so on!

Briefly reflect on the ease with which we pass judgement on others.

Living Scripture

1   Why did God call Hosea to marry an adulterous wife? **Note:** Commentators disagree about whether she was a woman who was already living an immoral life or one who would subsequently be unfaithful to him.

2   Couldn't Hosea just have spoken God's message? Was the tragedy of a broken marriage and rejected children – not all of whom might have been Hosea's! – really necessary? What difference does Hosea's rescue of Gomer (3:1–5) make?

3   When we read God's view of the human situation (11:1–11), what does that add to our understanding of God's instructions to Hosea?

4   God called Hosea to do something completely shocking. Doubtless respectable religious people would have condemned him. Jesus too was condemned as a friend of prostitutes and tax collectors. What implications does this have to the ways in which *we* relate to:-

—   people who lead a promiscuous lifestyle. (According to a BBC Radio 1 poll only 21 per cent of 16–24 year olds had only had one sexual partner in the previous year; 18 percent had had more than ten.)

—   gay people. Christians have been very defensive about government-introduced anti-discrimination legislation. Is opposition the only option for Bible-believing Christians?

5   How do we offer God's grace and forgiveness to people like Gomer who have willingly chosen slavery to an immoral lifestyle?

 Touching God

Making our vows
Using the wedding video that's been brought along, watch the part where the couple make their vows. Alternatively, get a copy of the marriage service and read the vows. Work together to create a form of words (and a ceremony if you wish) in which to renew your vows to God, or look at the wording your particular church or denomination uses for membership renewal, if it has a set service for this. As a starting point, you may wish to look at some of the prayers used by the United Reformed Church for their Rededication Sunday and given on page 46 (more at **www.urc.org.uk**). After creating it, make that act of renewal together.

Or

I'm sorry
Get hold of a copy of Bob Hartman's book *Telling the Bible* (different editions published by Lion Hudson and Monarch) and use the 'Hey That's OK' reading in the group.

And

Hearing from God
Take time to be quiet, listen to God, share what God gives, briefly discuss and record it.

Reaching out

Random acts of kindness

The idea behind **Random acts of kindness** is to do something kind for someone unconnected with you and completely out of the blue. See **www.actsofkindness.org** for lots of ideas. I don't know whether the originators of the idea are Christians but it's a pretty good example of grace. Activities they suggest include, for example, paying for the meal of the person next to you in the café queue; giving a collection of money-off coupons to someone. These acts can be very simple: opening a door for someone; letting the person behind you in the supermarket queue go ahead of you. Discuss ideas in the group and commit to carrying out some of them in the coming week.

Or

Apology needed?

Some Christians have travelled through Muslim countries to apologise for the Crusades. Martin Graham in his book *Sizzling Faith* (Kingsway, 2006) tells of how in a mission in Tonbridge he was led to apologise for the way the church had hurt the people of Tonbridge through an incident hundreds of years ago. The apology proved a breakthrough in the mission.

Consider how the church in your area might need to apologise to its community.

 ## Digging deeper

Encourage group members to share any journal entries from the past week. Before listening to God in the coming week, think of one person who has hurt you at some time and ask God to help you forgive them. Record your thoughts.

Postscript to group leaders

Hosea speaks very powerfully and directly about key issues. In most groups there are people who are hurting as a result of broken or damaged relationships. Be prepared to offer support, prayer and counsel.

Prayers of Rededication

taken from the United Reformed Church Rededication Service

Our Lord Jesus Christ prayed that all who came to believe in the Gospel might be one.
One in community and faith, one in witness and care.
As followers of Jesus we have failed time and again,
And so we make confession of those failures and seek God's forgiveness.

(Silence for reflection)

We have built up walls to divide the Body of Christ
And ignored its unity.
We have sinned, God forgive us.

We have dwelt upon what separates us,
And not sought what makes us one in the Body of Christ.
We have sinned, God forgive us.

We have belittled each other's gifts and traditions.
We have sinned, God forgive us.

We have not loved you, Lord,
As we find you in our brothers and sisters in Christ.
We have sinned, God forgive us.

Meditation

In my thoughts…
    He must increase, but I must decrease.
In my reading, listening and watching…
    He must increase, but I must decrease.
In my conversations…
    He must increase, but I must decrease.
In my relationships with family, friends and colleagues…
    He must increase, but I must decrease.
In the way that I do my work and exercise my responsibilities…
    He must increase, but I must decrease.
In my leisure time…
    He must increase, but I must decrease.
In my prayer life…
    He must increase, but I must decrease.
In my Bible reading and study…
    He must increase, but I must decrease.
In my worship…
    He must increase, but I must decrease.
In this group…
    He must increase, but I must decrease.

12 Amos: The prophet of social justice

Amos 2:6–16 and 5:1–17

A session exploring justice and worship

Amos was a shepherd, a southerner called by God to prophesy to the north. The northern kingdom of Israel was very religious. People packed into the religious centres. Sacrifices were continually offered. But it was based on shaky foundations. When the two kingdoms split (after Solomon), Jeroboam, the northern king, adapted the teaching of Moses to make Israel less dependent on Jerusalem (which was in the southern kingdom of Judah) and more authentically northern.

Two hundred years later the people thought everything was fine. But Amos – and God – thought differently. One of the key themes in Amos is that true worship must be worked out in holy living. And Israel was far from holy: the rich were getting richer and the poor were trampled underfoot. Incest, drunkenness and the pursuit of luxury and pleasure were its hallmarks. Justice was only available to those who could pay for it. It's not hard to see parallels with our world. So be ready in this session to allow God to challenge our values, our attitudes and our lifestyles.

 Getting connected

Fair taste

Start the evening with a Fair Trade blind coffee tasting. Make up a number of cups of coffee from different Fair Trade brands (and perhaps some non-Fair Trade too). Everyone should try each one, give a score and make comments about taste etc. After sharing the results, reveal which coffee is which. If you prefer, have tea tasting, chocolate tasting or wine tasting.

Or

Act the part

Role play a discussion between a farmer, a supermarket buyer and a customer. The farmer wants a reasonable return for his labour and investment; the supermarket buyer needs to be able to sell products at low prices in order to undercut his rivals while still making a profit for his shareholders; the customer wants cheap prices but also has some sense of social responsibility and maybe a desire for quality as well as cheapness.

 Living Scripture

1 Identify the crimes of which God accuses his people in Amos 2:6–8 and 5:11–13. What are the contemporary parallels?

2 Read Amos 4:1–5; 5:21–24 and 8:4–6,11,12. We often judge our church services on the quality of the music and the preaching. If God judges them according to whether we, as his people tolerate (or even practise) injustice, then how does he view our worship? Is it really true that our business lives, political lives and personal lives determine whether our worship is acceptable to God? What are the practical results of viewing worship in this light?

3 In Amos 7:10–17 we see the response of the political and religious powers to Amos' preaching. In what ways should the preaching and teaching of the Church interact with local,

national and international politics? What are the effects likely to be? How do we guard against becoming amateur politicians rather than witnesses for Christ?

4 On a scale of 1 (unimportant) to 5 (vital) how important is:

	My Score	Group Average Score
making an effort to buy fairly traded goods		
investing (for example, your pension) ethically		
writing to the media or business about social justice		
joining a campaign group		
getting personally involved with the developing world through activities such as a gap year or short-term mission		
giving financial support to agencies which promote social justice		
prayer alongside any or all of the above		
prayer on its own		

Hand out photocopies of this chart. Complete as individuals and then discuss the different priorities that emerge within the group. Calculate the average score and discuss further.

 Touching God

Affirm God's Word
Read aloud Amos 5:4–6. Open the curtains and look out on to the community or go out into the street or garden. Pray that God will move by his Holy Spirit to enable your community to seek him and live.

Together read aloud Amos 9:11–15. Thank God that ultimately his plans and purposes will be fulfilled. Thank him that there is mercy and grace for his people even though we fail him so often.

Or

Light a candle
You will need: a tray of sand and a number of small candles.

Place one small candle in the sand and light it. Draw the curtains and turn off the lights. Read aloud Amos 4:13. Seek God's forgiveness for the injustices that have brought darkness on our land. Then, after a period of silence, let each person take a candle, light it from the lit candle, and place it in the sand. As they do, they should mention one person or situation related to injustice and wrongdoing in the community, the country or the world.

When all the candles have been lit, look around the room and see the difference a lot of little lights have made. Praise God that in the midst of darkness he brings light into the world and that he does it through lots of little individuals who on their own would have hardly any effect. You might like to sing 'Light of the World' or 'Shine, Jesus, Shine'.

And

Hearing from God
Take time to be quiet, listen to God, share what God gives, briefly discuss and record it.

 Reaching out

Identify and act
Who are the most vulnerable in your community? Be creative in coming up with answers; don't just think of the obvious candidates. Is there anything the group could do for these people?

Or

Prayer walk
As a group go out and walk around your neighbourhood praying as you are prompted by the things you see. Ask God to help you be salt and light in your community. Prayer walking is not as conspicuous as it looks. If you keep your eyes open (good idea when you're walking!) and walk in twos or threes, then prayer looks just like conversation.

Or

Got the T-shirt
Decide together on a logo and slogan which would say something 'prophetic' about God's desire for justice in the world. Have T-shirts printed for the group and wear them in church. Listen to people's comments. Or perhaps you could have a lot of T-shirts printed and sell them in the church or elsewhere?

 Digging deeper

Encourage group members to share any journal entries from the past week. For the coming week, buy seven fairly traded food products. Each day, before you listen to God, read the label on one product and reflect on what was involved in its production and who produced it. Record your thoughts.

13 Malachi: The prophet of diversion and distraction

Malachi 2:10–16

A session about focusing on the task God has given and not being distracted

The author of this book is otherwise unknown. The name Malachi means 'my messenger'. The book was written about the time of Ezra and Nehemiah, perhaps just before Ezra came to Jerusalem around 458 BC. The great theme of Malachi is God's covenant (agreement) with his people. It's implicit in 1:2–5 and explicit in 4:4. But, far from responding positively to God's love, his people are apathetic, bored with worship and mean in their giving. God has called them to the great task of rebuilding their city and their temple – rebuilding their life and their faith. But they have allowed all sorts of distractions to get in the way. Through Malachi, God calls them back.

 Getting connected

Crime and punishment

> # Crime and punishment
>
> My object all sublime
>   I shall achieve in time –
> To let the punishment fit the crime –
>   The punishment fit the crime;
> And make each prisoner pent
>   Unwillingly represent
> A source of innocent merriment!
>   Of innocent merriment!
>
> *The Mikado,* Gilbert & Sullivan

What are the things in modern life that annoy you the most? For example, other people's loud conversations on mobile phones? If you could make the punishment fit the crime – create poetic justice for the perpetrators – what would it be? Would you condemn them always to hear the sound of their phone ringing but never be able to find it and answer it? Perhaps you could try to write a new verse for this song from *The Mikado.* Do we find it discouraging when people 'get away' with things we think are bad? What can we do?

Or

Promise you won't laugh

Ask a volunteer to read a passage from a book – not the Bible. The rest of the group should attempt (without speaking) to make the reader laugh. Repeat until bored! Discuss briefly how we cope with distractions.

Living Scripture

Before focusing on the specific passage, read the whole book aloud or silently. It takes about five minutes to read all three chapters of Malachi through aloud.

1 Malachi gives a number of examples of things that distract God's people from God himself and from the work that he has given them. From our perspective we happily label them as sin. I suspect the people of the time justified their actions as 'getting on with life' or 'making pragmatic decisions at a difficult time'. Before getting into the detail of one of those distractions (relationships) take a few moments to reflect silently on the question: Is there anything which I regard as a *necessary compromise* which others looking at my life might regard as serious sin which diverts me from God?

2 Read Malachi 2:10–16. Why was marriage to women of other races regarded as wrong? Was it just racism? Take a look at 1 Kings 11: 4–8 if you need a clue. Why was the marriage of Boaz (an Israelite) to Ruth (a Moabitess) OK if these marriages were not? Compare verse 11 with Ruth 1:16. What do you notice about Malachi's description of these foreign wives?

3 The returning exiles probably took extra wives from among the races living in the land for political or economic reasons (that is, to gain influence or land). When we act as if the end justifies the means, what does this say about our trust in God? Are there contemporary situations where we say, 'I know we shouldn't really do this but…' ?

4 Because they were unfaithful, God no longer paid attention to his people or accepted their offerings with pleasure (verse 13). How did they try to persuade God to answer their prayers? Why was this ineffective? Are there situations today where our prayers (individually or corporately) are not answered because we have broken faith with God?

5 God hates divorce (verse 16) but nevertheless permitted divorce (Deuteronomy 24:1–4) and even sometimes seems to command it (Ezra 10:1–4,10,11). How do you reconcile this?

6 Either

As openly as is appropriate for your group, share your experiences of the conflicting demands of your personal relationships and your relationships with God.

Or

Discuss: If you had to make a choice between your relationship with God and your relationship with someone else, what would be the key factors in your choice?

 Touching God

Distractions and the divine

Close your eyes. Listen carefully to the sounds in the room. Focus on the other people in the group. Can you hear people breathing? Can you hear individual people breathing? What other sounds can you hear? Use your memory to remember where people are sitting, what they are wearing and what they look like.

Repeat the exercise with a CD quietly playing music in the background. Does this help you to hear the other members of the group? Does it help you to picture them in your mind? Or is it a distraction?

Do the exercise once more, this time with a radio tuned to a channel of spoken word. What difference does this make?

Talk together about the things that enhance your focus on God and the things that distract:

- in your private prayers and Bible reading;

- in worship services;

- in small-group sessions.

Are there ways of using the distractions to bring you closer to God? What about the really big 'distractions' of life – family, career, church?

Close your eyes and listen again (with or without music according to whether most people found it helpful). Try turning each *distraction* you hear into a prayer. If you feel ambitious try it again with the radio on.

Or

Honesty or hypocrisy
You will need: a wide selection of the day's newspapers.

Tear out articles that seem to you to reflect blatant sin or hypocrisy. Spread them out on the floor of the room (or on a table) and look at them for a few minutes. Choose two or three and reflect on how the person committing the sin might seek to justify it. Look through the stories again. Choose one that reflects a temptation you face. The story is likely to be more extreme than your situation. For example, someone may have embezzled money from work while you may only wish you could lay your hands on a lot of money, no questions asked! Ask God silently to help you be honest about your own situation and its seriousness in damaging your relationship with God. Together as a group read aloud Psalm 32.

Or

Remembrance scrolls
You will need: a piece of parchment or hand-made paper for each person in the group (available from larger stationery stores, craft shops or online); gold and silver gel pens or calligraphy pens and coloured inks; about 20 cm of ribbon for each person.

Read Malachi 3:16. Using the paper in landscape format, list the names of each person in the group. Against each name write one positive characteristic of the person for which you thank God. Go around the group, with each sharing what you have written about the others.

Then each member should share one area of life where they would welcome help in focusing on God. Write these things onto the scrolls against each name.

Take time to pray together over these issues. Then roll up your remembrance scrolls, tying them with ribbon and take them home. Commit yourself to offering prayers of thanks and intercession for all the people in the scroll in your daily prayers for the coming week.

And

Hearing from God
Take time to be quiet, listen to God, share what God gives, briefly discuss and record it.

Reaching out

Prodigals

Make a list of people who used to be part of your church (maybe part of your small group) but who don't come any more. Some will be happily settled in other churches. For the rest, briefly consider why they stopped coming – but don't let this turn into a gossip session! Identify one or two people you can pray for and consider ways to invite them back into the life of the church.

 Digging deeper

Encourage group members to share any journal entries from the past week. For the coming week, here are some questions to ask as you prepare to listen to God, alongside some verses to look at – all from Malachi. Photocopy this list and give it to everyone to take home. Remind them to record their answers.

Day 1 – How much does God love me (1:2)?

Day 2 – Do I ever show contempt for God (1:6)?

Day 3 – Does my life cause others to stumble (2:8)?

Day 4 – Does God get tired of listening to me (2:17)?

Day 5 – Do I rob God (3:8)?

Day 6 – Do I moan about God (3:13)?

Day 7 – Am I ready for when Jesus returns (chapter 4)?

14 John the Baptist: The prophet from the wilderness

Luke 3:1–20 and 7:18–35

A session focusing on calling people to repentance and pointing to Jesus

Well in advance…

For **Locusts**, you will need to purchase some locusts for eating! They can be bought online (packs of 10, frozen) from **www.osgrow.co.uk**. This site has a recipe for stir-fry locusts which you could try or, apparently, they can be dipped in chocolate and eaten! Further research on the Internet reveals that locusts can also be barbecued on a skewer, roasted or fried. For a less adventurous eating experience, buy some honeycombs to share and taste.

After a long gap in which the voice of prophecy seems to have been silent, John the Baptist appeared, preaching in the wilderness. His dress, his lifestyle, his location and his message – all proclaimed him as a prophet. People flocked to hear him. All the prophets, in some way, pointed forward to Jesus. Yet John had the unique privilege of pointing people directly to Jesus in person. In preparing people to meet Jesus, he had a clear message – 'repent' – and he gave practical examples of how that should work out in practice.

Although he baptised Jesus and saw something of Jesus' ministry, even John (like Elijah) had his doubts; perhaps not surprising since he was imprisoned, having upset Herod by his forthright preaching. Jesus proclaimed John as the greatest of the prophets but the end of an era. From now on something new was to happen.

The time is now around AD 30.

 Getting connected

Locusts (Matthew 3:4)
You will need: locusts! (See **Well in advance…**)

This starter (sorry about the pun) is for the brave only! Cook and eat the locusts in whatever style you fancy. Talk afterwards about this new eating experience.

Or

The Wilderness Life Game
You will need: an A3 photocopy of **The Wilderness Life Game** from the centre spread of this book, pasted onto some card if possible; counters; dice.

Each person throws the dice, moves their counter and then follows the instructions on the square they land on.

 Living Scripture

Read Luke 3:1–20 and 7:18–35

1 John was neither polite nor tactful in his preaching (3:7–9). If the message the Church brings today doesn't upset people, does that mean it has lost its cutting edge?

2 Examples are given of John's preaching to three different groups of people (3:12–17). What would be their contemporary equivalents and what would John say to them? What would John say to us?

3 John was eventually imprisoned for speaking too directly about the moral and political issues of his day (3:19,20). Are there issues today where Christians ought to risk imprisonment or anger rather than keep quiet?

4 John's chief aim was to point people to Jesus (3:15–18). How can the Church balance a message of practical repentance which of necessity will involve us in political and social controversy and still point people to Jesus?

5 John was the greatest of all the prophets (7:28), but he lived in the period of promise. Christians live in the period of fulfilment – and hence are greater than John and therefore greater (that is, in a more privileged position) than any of the prophets. Pause to think about the implications of that for a few moments. If this is so, then what does it say about our responsibilities?

6 John was marked out as a prophet partly by his lack of concern for the things the world regards as important (7:24–26). Can we be faithful to our prophetic calling as disciples of Jesus and yet live the same lifestyle and hold the same values as those around us?

 Touching God

Increase and decrease
Use the meditation on page 46. A different person in turn reads each line. The whole group responds with the words in bold italics. One option would be to allow some time for anyone to add in other areas of life at the end, following the same pattern.

And

Hearing from God
Take time to be quiet, listen to God, share what God gives, briefly discuss and record it.

 Reaching out

Baptism
Find out more about baptism. If your church practises believers' baptism (immersion in water as a public declaration of belief in Christ), invite someone from a church that practises infant baptism or christening to share their understanding with the group. And vice versa. Look for an opportunity to attend a baptism that is different from your own custom. What prophetic messages does the symbolism of baptism convey?

Or

Sort and share
Look at Luke 3:11 together. Decide on a way to share from your abundance. You could sort through your wardrobes and cupboards and make a collection of clothes and other items that

could be taken to a charity shop. Or give food to your local soup kitchen, mission or refuge. Or sell some surplus possessions on eBay and give the money raised to charity.

Or

Pressure at work

Find out something about the pressures faced by Christians in different occupations. If you can identify a specific group such as Christians in education or health care or local government, why not organise a prayer breakfast for them to provide support and encouragement?

 ## Digging deeper

Encourage group members to share any journal entries from the past week. For the coming week, suggest that group members repeat two or three times before each listening session: 'He must increase, but I must decrease.' Record your thoughts.

15 Barnabas, Simeon, Lucius, Manaen and Saul: Prophecy in the Church

Acts 13:1–3

A session about prophecy in the church in New Testament times and today

Well in advance...

You may feel that the topic of prophecy today may be a little daunting or complex to be tackling in a small group. If you'd like to do some research ahead of time, then the following books may be helpful:

– For a popular-level approach to spiritual gifts today that includes a helpful and practical chapter on prophecy, try *Know Your Spiritual Gifts*, Mark Stibbe (Marshall Pickering, 2000).

– For a more detailed survey, there is a lot of good material in *Systematic Theology*, Wayne Grudem (IVP, 1994).

– There is also a condensed version of this book (easier to read – cheaper to buy!) published as *Bible Doctrine*, Wayne Grudem (IVP, 1999).

Mike's diary, Tuesday 25 September 2006:

Staff team meeting at Mutley Baptist Church, Plymouth. I shared with the team that I was having a problem writing the final session of Multi-Sensory Prophets. I couldn't find a passage of Scripture to base it on. As Alison prayed that I would find a passage, I not only knew that it should be Acts 13... but I could see how the session would develop.

So does what happened – as recorded in my diary snippet – make this a better, more spiritual, more God-given session than the rest of them? I don't think so. But it is a reminder that although God often uses our gifts and skills, our memory and learning, and a whole host of natural processes, sometimes he speaks very directly in answer to prayer – or even sometimes when we are not expecting it at all.

The context of our Scripture passage is that the church leaders at Antioch were meeting around 36 AD.

 Getting connected

Brainstorm

How many prophets are mentioned by name in the Bible? Brainstorm as many as you can think of. (Herbert Lockyer, in *All the Messianic Prophecies of the Bible,* Zondervan, 1973, lists 40 different men and 5 women who are named as prophets.)

Or

Twenty questions

Working in pairs, one person thinks of something true and interesting about themselves that the other person is unlikely to know. The second person can ask 20 questions with the aim of discovering the secret, to which only the answers 'yes' and 'no' may be given. Repeat, reversing the roles.

 Living Scripture

1   Read Acts 13:1–3. Which of the five church leaders at Antioch was a prophet? Through which of them did this prophecy come? When did the prophecy come? What is Luke telling us about prophecy in the Church in what he omits and what he includes here?

2   This prophecy only had relevance to the church at Antioch, and particularly for Barnabas and Saul. Their obedience to the prophecy, though, had much wider implications. Should we look to God to speak to us about immediate and local issues ('Send this person… ', 'Start this ministry… ', 'Go to this place… ') or should we look to God to give us prophetic words for the nation or the whole world? Check out other examples in Acts where God speaks in a very direct way: 10:9–16; 16:6–10; 21:7–11.

3   How does Paul explain the purpose of prophecy and regulate its use? In 1 Corinthians 14 he is contrasting it with speaking in tongues. Either read the whole chapter or focus on verses 1–5,12,22–25,29–32,39,40.

4   Potentially, every Christian can prophesy (Acts 2:17). What implications does this have for our

   – services of worship?

   – prayer meetings?

   – small groups?

   – church committee meetings?

5   Read 1 Thessalonians 5:19-22. In a few sentences (write them out on a flip chart or large sheet of paper) try to summarise what you have discovered through all the sessions you've studied. Try to answer these key questions:

   – What is prophecy?

   – Who can prophesy?

   – What safeguards against false prophecy should be in place? If you did not look at 1 John way back in the first session (**Living Scripture** question 2) it might be helpful to look at it now.

   – What place does/could/should prophecy have in today's Church?

   – What place could/should prophecy have in my life?

 Touching God

Times past

Read together the extracts on page 61 about a preacher of a previous generation, at a time when prophetic gifts were largely regarded as having ceased. Are these examples of God speaking prophetically? Share any instances of sermons you have heard where God spoke directly to you in a way that was beyond what the preacher could have known. How did you respond? What happened? Pray prayers of thanksgiving for God's direct input into your life. Pray prayers of intercession for all the preachers you know.

Note: Some people may say that these extracts are 'words of knowledge' (see 1 Corinthians 14:6). Try not to get sidetracked arguing about terms. The important question is whether God is speaking supernaturally; and in this case does God speak through preachers more than they consciously know? If you do want to explore the different ways in which God speaks, then see the books mentioned under **Well in advance…**

Or

Blowing bubbles
Use this idea to close the series, so if you are going to have an extra session (see **Final postscript** below) then use this idea at the end of it.

You will need: some plastic pots of bubble mix with wands (one for each person). If you can get hold of one of the children's toys that blows really big bubbles that would be good.

Let everyone have fun blowing bubbles. Then together get as many bubbles in the air at once as you can. As you watch them pop read together Matthew 24:35. Thank God for all he has revealed through these sessions and pray that he will go on speaking through his Word and that we will have ears to hear.

And

Hearing from God
Take time to be quiet, listen to God, share what God gives, briefly discuss and record it. Look back through the notes you have made and see what God has been saying to the group. Thank him for his grace and faithfulness. Check out whether there are things you need to do in response to what you have heard.

 ## Reaching out

Eat well
Prepare and share a meal together to mark the end of your studies about prophets. If you have space, invite guests to join you and in the conversation around the table(s) share what God has been saying to you.

And/Or

Weekend away
Plan a weekend away together to continue exploring how God speaks into our lives and what the implications of that are for us. You could try a centre that provides guided retreats or plan and run your own programme.

 ## Digging deeper

Encourage group members to share any journal entries from the past week. Ask everyone to put special emphasis on listening carefully to what other people say to them each day. Focus on hearing God through others. Take some time alone later and record your thoughts.

Final postscript to group leaders

To give yourself time to reflect on what God has been saying through the group sessions and to share what you have recorded in your journals you may find it helpful to have an additional session without a fixed programme. Choose any **Getting connected** idea and any **Touching God** idea that you haven't previously used, but spend most of the time sharing together. Don't forget to include some listening time. Finish with the **Blowing bubbles** activity as described above.

Encourage team members not to stop at that! Suggest the group continues to include time for listening to God regularly in your group meetings, whatever topic you may be studying. If some in the group have found the habit of journalling helpful, urge them to buy a small notebook and maintain the habit of listening to God and recording the significant things that happen in their day.

TIMES PAST

C H Spurgeon was the most famous and widely heard preacher of the Victorian era. These are some of the stories told about his preaching.

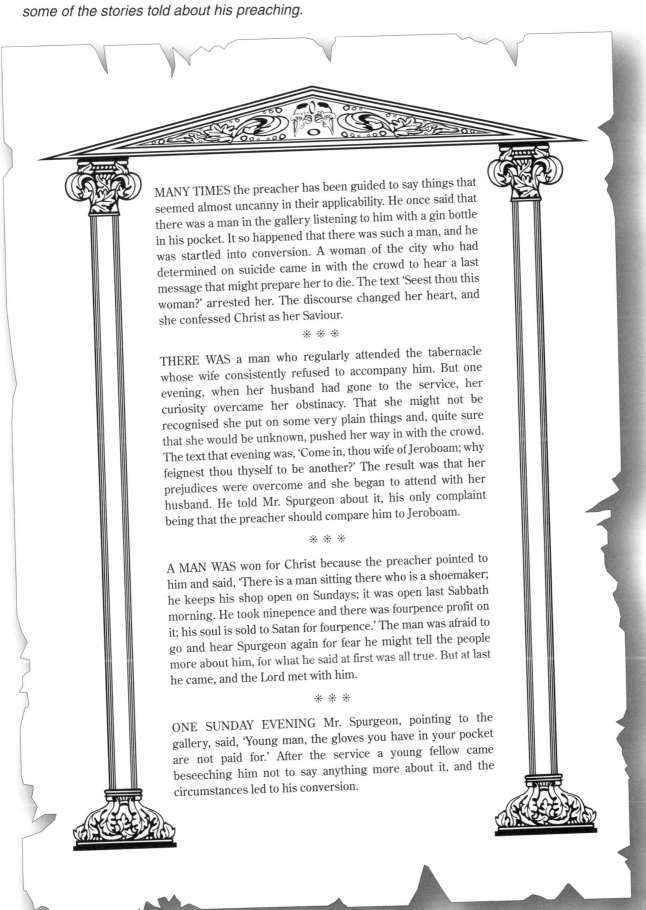

MANY TIMES the preacher has been guided to say things that seemed almost uncanny in their applicability. He once said that there was a man in the gallery listening to him with a gin bottle in his pocket. It so happened that there was such a man, and he was startled into conversion. A woman of the city who had determined on suicide came in with the crowd to hear a last message that might prepare her to die. The text 'Seest thou this woman?' arrested her. The discourse changed her heart, and she confessed Christ as her Saviour.

* * *

THERE WAS a man who regularly attended the tabernacle whose wife consistently refused to accompany him. But one evening, when her husband had gone to the service, her curiosity overcame her obstinacy. That she might not be recognised she put on some very plain things and, quite sure that she would be unknown, pushed her way in with the crowd. The text that evening was, 'Come in, thou wife of Jeroboam; why feignest thou thyself to be another?' The result was that her prejudices were overcome and she began to attend with her husband. He told Mr. Spurgeon about it, his only complaint being that the preacher should compare him to Jeroboam.

* * *

A MAN WAS won for Christ because the preacher pointed to him and said, 'There is a man sitting there who is a shoemaker; he keeps his shop open on Sundays; it was open last Sabbath morning. He took ninepence and there was fourpence profit on it; his soul is sold to Satan for fourpence.' The man was afraid to go and hear Spurgeon again for fear he might tell the people more about him, for what he said at first was all true. But at last he came, and the Lord met with him.

* * *

ONE SUNDAY EVENING Mr. Spurgeon, pointing to the gallery, said, 'Young man, the gloves you have in your pocket are not paid for.' After the service a young fellow came beseeching him not to say anything more about it, and the circumstances led to his conversion.

Extracted from *C H Spurgeon, A Biography*, W Y Fullerton, Williams & Norgate, 1920

Listening to God

Journal

Name:

Date:

Getting the most out of your journal

— Take your journal to the group meetings; make a note of what you are asked to focus on for the week.

— Carry the journal with you as often as you can.

— Write brief notes concerning the thoughts that come to you when you pray and read the Bible.

— Note any other thoughts that occur at other times as you interact with your world.

— At the next group session be ready to share (if appropriate) the notes you have made.

Listening to God
Journal

Week beginning:

Day 4:

Day 5:

Day 6:

Day 7:

Listening to God
Journal

Week beginning:

Focus for the week:

Day 1:

Day 2:

Day 3:

Other books in the Multi-Sensory series

✳ fresh ✳ innovative ✳ imaginative ✳ inspirational ✳ practical

MULTI-SENSORY CHURCH

Over 30 ready-to-use ideas for creative churches and small groups

Sue Wallace

MULTI-SENSORY PRAYER

Over 60 ready-to-use ideas for creative churches and small groups

Sue Wallace

MULTI-SENSORY SCRIPTURE

50 innovative ideas for exploring the Bible in churches and small groups

Sue Wallace

MULTI-SENSORY TOGETHER

15 ready-to-use sessions for Bible exploration in creative small groups

Ian Birkinshaw

MULTI-SENSORY SEASONS

15 ready-to-use Bible-based sessions through the seasons for creative small groups

Wendy Rayner and Annie Slade

MULTI-SENSORY PARABLES

15 ready-to-use sessions on the stories Jesus told – for creative churches and small groups

Ian Birkinshaw

This series is just part of a wide range of resources for churches and small groups published by Scripture Union. There's also a free online magazine about the world of small groups called church@home. Go to **www.scriptureunion.org.uk/churchathome**

SU publications are available from Christian bookshops, on the Internet or via mail order. You can:

- –   phone SU's mail order line: 0845 0706006
- –   email info@scriptureunion.org.uk
- –   log on to www.scriptureunion.org.uk
- –   write to SU Mail Order, PO Box 5148, Milton Keynes MLO, MK2 2YX